On Being Indian

Literary Activism

Series Editor: Amit Chaudhuri

On Being Indian

The Organic Intellectual,
Mystical Poetry, and Lineages of
Indian Rationalism

Amit Chaudhuri

First published by Westland Books, a division of Nasadiya Technologies Private Limited, in 2023

No. 269/2B, First Floor, 'Irai Arul', Vimalraj Street, Nethaji Nagar, Alapakkam Main Road, Maduravoyal, Chennai 600095

Westland and the Westland logo are the trademarks of Nasadiya Technologies Private Limited, or its affiliates.

Copyright © Amit Chaudhuri, 2023

Amit Chaudhuri asserts the moral right to be identified as the author of this work.

ISBN: 9789357767934

10 9 8 7 6 5 4 3 2 1

The views and opinions expressed in this work are the author's own and the facts are as reported by them and the publisher is in no way liable for the same.

All rights reserved

Typeset by Jojy Philip, New Delhi 110 015

Printed at Parksons Graphics Pvt. Ltd

No part of this book may be reproduced, or stored in a retrieval system, or transmitted in any form or by any means, electronic, mechanical, photocopying, recording, or otherwise, without express written permission of the publisher.

A Note on the Series

'Literary activism' is a project that began in 2014 with a series of annual symposia. Its aim was to create a space for the kind of discussion on creativity no longer available in mainstream contexts (literary festivals, book launches) or in academic ones (conferences, classrooms, monographs). The literary activism website—literaryactivism.com—was created in 2020, and Centre for the Creative and the Critical at Ashoka University came into existence in 2022 at Ashoka University to give this project a home, and to look at the kind of thinking that writing and the arts comprise.

This new imprint, 'literary activism', is meant to carry forward these ambitions in the realm of publishing. The art vs science debate is now a historical relic, but what interests us is the possibility of creating a meaning for writing that's separate from market value and academic legitimacy. And we wish to recall that art and writing are not synonymous with the generalised academic discipline called the 'humanities': they have an angularity to it, and to the social science perspectives the humanities are now subsumed under. The 'literary activism' imprint wishes not only to publish good writing, but to pursue this angularity.

IN THESE PAGES, I'M GOING BACK TO A PARTICULAR time to record certain events that happened then. That makes it seem like I'm talking about something that happened decades ago. But what I wish to do is go back about three years.

I was in Paris for roughly nine months in 2018–19. The fellowship that had taken me there—to a rented flat in a West African neighbourhood, in a building on the fragrantly named Rue des Poissonniers—was ending. My daughter was with me in the second half of May, visiting from London, where she too was coming to the end of something: a BA in comparative literature. She spent a lot of time in the Paris apartment finishing two final-year theses. I poked my nose into them and learnt that one of them was on the 'organic intellectual'. The term was a discovery for me. I asked my daughter what it meant, but she was evasive, because she thought I was quizzing her and also because she was busy. As I attempted to grasp its meaning, I became aware of the vagueness of its provenance. It had been invented by Antonio Gramsci, but it's not as if Gramsci had written a great deal about it. In fact, tracing it to the pertinent sections in the *Prison Notebooks* wasn't easy. The term had been invoked and defined relatively briefly, and then taken on a life of its own, in the way that the passing reference in the *Phaedo*, to the fact that Socrates had turned to music before his death, had for Nietzsche.

This period in Rue des Poissonniers was poised between stasis (my daughter bent over her laptop) and speed (her rapid movement across the keyboard). It was also when, in India, 'revelations were at hand'. The Bharatiya Janata Party (BJP) and its satellites in the National Democratic Alliance (NDA) had returned for a second term in India with—so we were told from 23rd May onwards—37.7 per cent of the vote and 303 seats in the parliament. This meant a substantial portion of the electorate (not the majority, but enough to contribute crucially to the distribution of seats under India's parliamentary system) had given the NDA (effectively, the BJP) carte blanche in governance.

One term of the BJP would mean, we knew in 2014, a shift towards Hindu fantasy and kitsch utopianism: cow urine as medicine, astrology as science, the flying chariots in the Ramayana serving as evidence of the ancient Indian mastery of aerodynamics, and Ganesha's elephant head as proof of our long-standing practice of plastic surgery. (Little attention would be paid, naturally, to India's path-breaking history in science and mathematics.) These absurdities of thought were hardly characteristic of India, but the BJP made sure they were dominant. They would be accompanied, in the first term, by recurrent violence towards Muslims, mainly in north India; a recasting of dissent as 'anti-national activity' and an entirely opportunistic use of the colonial law that had been invented to suppress sedition; and the forceful reinvention of certain north Indian greetings, like Jai Shri Ram (victory to Rama) and patriotic declamations coined during the freedom struggle or afterwards (Jai Hind, victory to

India; Bharat Mata ki Jai, victory to Mother India), as constant proclamations, and tests, of allegiance, a feverish rehabilitation of patriotic feeling that had begun in the 1980s with the slogan 'garv se kaho hum Hindu hain' ('declare proudly "We're Hindu"').

The first term was also the playground in which the BJP should have exhibited its prowess in free-market capitalism, unleashing on the world an India that would become the largest economy in just over a decade. Instead, the economy was damaged badly by a programme called 'demonetisation'. All this had energised and enlarged—in a way no study can account for—Narendra Modi's constituency.

What would the second term bring? The violent, symbolic utopianism to do with temples and cows would surely continue, but people feared, even in the first days of the election results' aftermath, that there would now be a radical makeover of the foundations—democracy, the judiciary, and the Constitution among them—of the nation state. That this would be the case was established briskly.

First came, at the end of July, the outlawing of a pernicious practice governed by Sharia law: 'triple talaq', or divorce accomplished by a man saying *talaq talaq talaq* to his wife. Talaq had been one of the main issues at the heart of the BJP's rise in the early 1980s from a non-viable party to a national one: the Congress had been unable to side with the Supreme Court's favourable ruling for a Muslim woman, Shah Bano Begum, who had questioned talaq in court, leading to a hardening among Hindus about their Muslim countrymen. This right-wing sentiment was nourished, not so much by the talaq issue, as by the perceived inability to integrate Muslims under the 'uniform civil code' and the putative appeasement of minorities (the word is a euphemism for Muslims) by successive governments. In India—possibly the most complex democratic system in the world, with countless centres of interest—it has always been difficult to have consensus about reform. Muslim women's groups had long asked for an end to triple talaq; what was spectacular was how quickly this matter was brought to the newly formed parliament's attention. This alacrity was disquieting because, after all, the bill was not being pushed through by a reformist government. This was a government that not only allowed a whole host of caste-related iniquities to flourish, but also was busy inventing new obscurantist practices itself—banning cow slaughter, for instance, in a way unrelated to concerns with animal or human welfare. The triple talaq bill became, then, not an instance of Enlightenment-style reform—the type of reform that once may have been liberatory in its intentions and yet in some ways open to the charge of insensitivity to cultural specificity—nor a measure taken by a government for which women's welfare had ever seemed a priority. It seemed simply like an opportunity taken to swiftly identify, single out, and corner a subset of the population.

A few days later, on 5th August 2019, a law was passed abrogating Article 370 of the Indian Constitution, which had, since 1952, given special status to the state of Jammu and Kashmir, granting it a degree of autonomy in matters of governance, the ownership of property, and residency. Article 370 was the outcome of negotiations leading up to and following the complex circumstances of its accession, as a Muslim-majority princely state ruled by a Hindu king, to India at the time of independence. This special status—made meaningless, anyway, over time, by decades of Kashmiri separatism (often Pakistan-fuelled) and Indian military intervention with its attendant atrocities—was now revoked for this troublesome and divisive region. Kashmir fell off the map, for it ceased being an Indian state and became a union territory directly governed by New Delhi. Its political leaders were jailed or put under house arrest, travel to and from the territory stopped, curfews were imposed, and phone and internet services were withdrawn. The swiftness with which the bill was passed and the measures that immediately followed were meant to hijack Kashmir and frighten the rest of India. These developments—alongside the spectacle of Enforcement Directorate officials climbing over walls to get into the former finance minister's house to fish him out and transfer him to jail, and the steady stream of academics and activists arrested for some version of abetment to insurgency—coalesced to create what the BJP appeared to want to be the dominant mood in its second term: fear.

On 11th December that year, the Citizenship Amendment Bill—meant to grant refuge and, eventually, citizenship to those seeking asylum on grounds of religious persecution from neighbouring countries, *as long as they weren't Muslim*—was passed into law by the parliament once the anguished speeches from the opposition had been heard. The resulting Citizenship Amendment Act (CAA) was significant because of the resumption in Assam of a massive, ultimately nationwide, project to do with the identification and, of course, displacement of those who had been in India as 'illegal' immigrants (that is, Muslims from Bangladesh) since 1951: the creation of the National Register of Citizens (NRC).

One might say that the CAA was the first crystallisation of xenophobic national policy in a global context in which xenophobia had been on the boil for some time, whether it was the panic over Syrian refugees, Trump's 'America First' policies, or the referendum vote for Brexit, which would be achieved the following year. Xenophobia had received a fresh and significant lease on life from 9/11, after which hostility to Islam became normalised in the globalised mainstream. But what does 'global' in the phrase 'global rise in xenophobia' mean? 'Global' was, from 1989 onwards, capitalism's celebratory word for the triumph of the market. What does it mean in the context of violence? One of the means of normalising xenophobia in the last twenty years has been the post-9/11 reaffirmation in the time of globalisation of an entity called the 'West', where the 'West' represents the history of democracy and free speech. These are taken to be synonymous with 'Western values'. This account is a betrayal of the way the right to be different and the right to dissent comprise human values that were shaped, and fought for, globally.

The anti-CAA protests and their uniqueness—the fact that their agenda was humanity itself, and that so many who believed in humanity participated in the protests—remind us, among other things, of the limitation of 'Western values' in containing xenophobia and, in its exclusionary version of the idea of liberty, its complicity with the xenophobic.

I HAD BEEN TRYING TO GET A CLEARER IDEA OF THE organic intellectual since the end of May 2019, and found I had to piece together a picture from stray quotations. The word 'intellectual' has hardly any meaning any more, because the non-institutional context intellectuals located themselves in, and contributed to, is no longer respected or even comprehended. What we have today is the academic whose intellectual oppositionality is shaped by professionalisation; that is, it has to adhere closely to prevalent disciplinary positions on politics. I would contrast the present-day 'professionalised' intellectual with erstwhile intellectual positions that were not so much individualistic as eccentric or unassimilable.

Then there is the American term 'public intellectual', which comes with its own previously determined definition, wherein the 'public intellectual' must make interventions that are comprehensible to the way the terms of the debate are set already.

Unsure about what 'intellectual' meant anymore, I began to find out a bit about what Gramsci thought of the category. The clearest, most persuasive articulation occurs negatively: the 'intellectual' is *not* to be confused with the 'organic intellectual'. We learn here of Gramsci's conception of what intellectuals are: a class of thinkers (comprising scholars, writers, and artists) that deems itself unaffiliated to class. Intellectuals might write or debate on class, but they aren't primarily defined by it: they are defined by their location in the intellectual tradition. The 'organic intellectual', on the other hand, *is* defined by class, by the economy, by profession (in a way quite different from academic professionalisation), and by their work. Valeriano Ramos Jr had this to say in 1982 about Gramsci's comparison:

> Traditional intellectuals are those intellectuals linked to tradition and to past intellectuals; those who are not so directly linked to the economic structure of their particular society and, in fact, conceive of themselves as having no basis in any social class and adhering to no particular class discourse or political discourse. Organic intellectuals, on the other hand, are more directly related to the economic structure of their society

> simply because of the fact that 'every social group that originates in the fulfilment of an essential task of economic production' creates its own organic intellectual. (Ramos 1982)

The term kept coming back to me, as a problem not fully sorted out, as something recurrent and half-remembered. It is not clear to me, from what I've read of Gramsci's formulations and others' formulations on those formulations, what relation the organic intellectual—the blue- or white-collar worker, say—has to what Gramsci called 'hegemony', and whether they disturb or protect it. What's available on the subject doesn't make this clear. Yet the term, maybe because of this lack of complete clarity, began to take on a new life for me in the last months of 2019 and, possibly, a new meaning. Its accidental discovery, as my daughter put together her thesis, became part of a resurrection in the midst of rising xenophobia.

Towards the end of July, as the outlawing of triple talaq was being put in place under the newly elected NDA government, a tweet (from 31st July 2019) concerning Zomato, a food delivery service, gives us a sense of the general atmosphere in which these 'reforms' were happening: 'Just cancelled an order on @ZomatoIN they allocated a non hindu rider for my food they said they can't change rider and can't refund on cancellation I said you can't force me to take a delivery I don't want don't refund just cancel.' (*Hindustan Times* 2020) The person from whom this stream-of-consciousness statement emanated identified himself as Amit Shukla of Jabalpur. This tweet was then retweeted by Zomato with the comment, 'Food doesn't have a religion. It is a religion.' For me, this isn't an observation that's secular in either the European sense (religion is a private matter; it has no place in the national or public domain) or in that of the Indian Constitution (the nation state is secular and non-religious, which also involves it being home to a multiplicity of worldviews, including those of different religions). Zomato's tweet—its phrasing—is more akin to a form of poetic, mystical dissent which suggests that the nature of the sacred is never settled. It is less interested in delineating the territories of the religious and the non-religious (the secular) than in claiming that anything could be sacred: 'It is a religion.' For something or someone to 'have' a religion is for them to follow a denomination; for something to 'be' a religion is for it to, at a given point of time, possess the quality of sacredness. The poet Arun Kolatkar explored this line of thinking, which he traced to mystics like Chaitanya, when he visited a largely disused (at the time) pilgrimage town, Jejuri. What has been abandoned, or even damaged ('scratched'), is made sacred in the eponymous poem-sequence from 1970 (Kolatkar 2005, 6, 22): 'no more a place of worship this / is nothing less than the house of god' ('Heart of Ruin'); 'scratch a rock / and a legend springs' ('A Scratch'). It is this renovating assignation of meaning that the phrasing of the Zomato tweet echoes, rather than a conventional secular piety.

The tweet may or may not have come from Zomato India's co-founder Deepinder Goyal. But he tweeted separately: 'We are proud of the idea of India—and the diversity of our esteemed customers and partners. We aren't sorry to lose any business that comes in the way of our values.' (*Times of India* 2019) This is less aphoristic than the Zomato tweet, but its rebuttal contains comparable paradoxes. The 'idea of India'—as a place, even a cliché, of immemorial diversity—takes on an oppositional resonance in the tweet, through what can only be called a political use of a marketing slogan. 'India is diverse and multifarious' has been the basis of many marketing campaigns in tourism. Here, the statement, with its reassuring reference to 'esteemed customers', seems part of that larger marketing-nationalist language of diversity while it actually comprises a riposte. There is a segue, in the plainer second sentence, from the upbeat multicultural slogans of free-market globalisation (expressed through coinages like the 'global village') into an incongruous, anti-marketing idealism: 'We aren't sorry to lose any business that comes in the way of our values.'

'Is it possible to classify this Zomato guy as an "organic intellectual"?' I asked my daughter.

THE ANTI-CAA PROTESTS BEGAN IN ASSAM ON 19TH December, just over a week after the act was passed by the parliament. The Assam protests happened on a scale beyond anything India had seen since 2014, when the BJP came to power, and it was certainly unprecedented in a second term marked by a series of punitive transformations. Although they were propelled not by a revulsion at the act's astonishingly upfront exclusion of Muslims from its list of refugees eligible for citizenship but more by Assam's longstanding internal demographic conflicts, the protests proved that citizens' movements could have a powerful life even in the BJP's India. Protests had spread to universities in other cities: Jamia Millia Islamia in New Delhi, Jawaharlal Nehru University (already struggling under the BJP/NDA regime), also in Delhi, and Aligarh Muslim University. These were clearly directed at the CAA's 'unconstitutional' discrimination along religious lines—its significant attempt to undermine India's Constitution.

The response from the police was retributive. But protests then began to grip entire cities in a way that couldn't be attributed to political parties or even to a particular political leader (in comparison, say, to Jayaprakash Narayan's role in mobilising mass dissent towards the end of the Emergency in 1977).

Huge, galvanised, spontaneous processions began to take place, involving an entity that was fragmentary, disunited, even putative—the Indian citizenry. I hadn't seen this sort of nationwide awakening anywhere in my own lifetime. All the movements I had seen close-up or from afar had a relationship to some kind of political leadership. Here, you felt the political parties in the opposition were onlookers who tried to revitalise their own formations by coming into contact with the protesters. Only the occasional anti-anti CAA protests were politically affiliated.

Then, gender and religion—and a heterogeneity of generations—came together in the anti-CAA protests by Muslim women (most of them in burqa) in an area called Shaheen Bagh in Delhi over that winter. Shaheen Bagh turned into the first site of civil disobedience by wives, grandmothers, and daughters who became immoveable until the pandemic came along; it was also the site of political and cultural play, of speeches, performances, and cups of tea. These gatherings were then replicated in other cities, including Calcutta, where, in the historically Muslim-dominated Park Circus neighbourhood, a twenty-minute walk from where I live, women congregated in the open air and stayed overnight, remaining as an encampment in the park for over a month, taking turns to replenish their own numbers as some returned temporarily to work or housework. Since West Bengal wasn't a BJP-ruled state, the women were, in time, allowed by the state government to set up portable toilets and tents to keep out the cold.

OVER THE YEARS, THE BJP HAS COINED SEVERAL TERMS to categorise the left-liberal, protesting students or, indeed, any kind of dissenter. 'Pseudo-secular' had, by 2019, an established history, going back to well before the BJP's first term; 'libtard' had been imported more recently into Indian discourse. The most widely used pejoratives were variations of 'anti-national'; for instance, 'Urban Naxal', where 'Naxal' referred to Maoists who had been a disruptive, revolutionary force (mainly in Bengal) in the late 1960s and who had had a resurgence in remote, neglected regions in India during the time of globalisation. The metaphor 'urban' was meant to indicate that the so-called urban Naxals were people who belonged to academia and elite milieus in cities and who were Naxals metaphorically, not literally, but were no less dangerous or reprehensible for that. An urban Naxal is possibly, in a certain political incarnation, close to Gramsci's idea of the intellectual, as one who perceives themselves less in terms of their own class (though their discourse may have to do with caste and class) than the intellectual lineage they belong to (in this case, a Left lineage). The word 'urban' would have been brought in by whoever coined this term to point to the class location of the intellectual. In conjunction with each other, 'urban' and 'Naxal' meant 'elite anti-national'.

Late 2019 to early 2020, however, saw interventions from figures who couldn't be identified as intellectuals in either a loose or specific sense. Kannan Gopinathan, an officer in the Indian Administrative Service—that is, the Indian civil service—resigned in August 2019 with the abrogation of Article 370 and Kashmir being put under quasi-military rule. Gopinathan, thirty-four years old at the time, was already known for his selfless work during the 2018 Kerala floods, when he acted beyond his role as an IAS officer. He resigned from the IAS on 21st August 2019 because he felt that 'we got into service because we felt we can provide voice to people, but then we ended up with our own voice taken away from us'. The matter of his 'voice' was on his mind because of Kashmir. On 24 August, he told the *Hindu*:

> Over the past few days, I have been really perturbed by what is happening in the country, wherein a large section of our population have had their fundamental rights suspended. There has been a lack of response to it. We seem to be perfectly fine with it. I also see in some small ways how I am also a part of it. I think if I had a newspaper, the only thing I would be printing on the front page would be '19' on the front page, because today is the nineteenth day. (Praveen 2019)

Gopinathan has since been asked—or threatened—by the government (which never processed his resignation) to get back to pandemic-related work, but he has neither gone back to the IAS nor joined politics as Indians often expect of those who are setting themselves up as idealists.

He was of interest because of the concern that institutions and administration—all that kept the 'miracle' of India functional—were entirely compromised, and that these institutions and instruments of governance seemed, in Gopinathan's words, 'to be perfectly fine with' this fact (at least outwardly). Having taken the step he had, Gopinathan became of interest to intellectuals, though he himself didn't become one in the conventional sense. He voluntarily fell out of the system, but remains, I think, marked by the system and its original vision of what might best emerge from it. Born in Kottayam district in Kerala, the son of an upper-division clerk in the Kerala government, educated in Palakkad district and Kottayam, he 'topped' the state-level Kerala Technical High School Leaving Certificate Examination and then later moved to Noida in Delhi, becoming closer than he'd been before to the centre of things. I would say that the potential idealism of the system—the reasons an independent nation state was fought for and created in the first place—finds a voice in Gopinathan in a very different way from a particular kind of liberal intellectual dissent (which, at times, and on some level, has long colluded with the state). From Gopinathan's example, one might assume that the 'organic intellectual' may fall out with—and from—the state, but not abandon it.

AMONG THE TERMS THE BJP HAD COINED SINCE 2014 to categorise all who opposed it politically as secessionists and seditionists was the Hinglish pejorative 'tukde-tukde gang'. 'Tukde tukde' is Hindi for 'bits and pieces' or 'fragments', and is generally used in sentences to describe cutting or breaking something into pieces: in this case, India. The term was reinvigorated periodically by the BJP. For instance, Home Minister Amit Shah said at a political rally in Delhi on 26th December 2019 that the anti-CAA protests were being propelled by the 'tukde-tukde gang' (https://www.youtube.com/watch?v=yQBk0HDnZys). He meant students and activists.

In the meantime, Saket Gokhale, described these days as an activist but not really present in the public consciousness at the time as one, put in a Right to Information (RTI) enquiry with the government asking it to disclose the names of the members of the tukde-tukde gang. His reasoning was that the gang should have members if it did indeed exist. The Right to Information Act had been put in place in 2005 after sustained work by activists. It gave the Indian citizen the right to request information from any public authority (that is, any state or governmental organisation) and expect a response within thirty days. In July 2019, the Right to Information (Amendment) Bill made an attempt to dilute the Act. On 20th January 2020, Gokhale tweeted that the Home Ministry had responded to his RTI query with: 'Ministry of Home Affairs has no information concerning tukde-tukde gang.' Gokhale then concluded that 'the "tukde-tukde gang" does not officially exist & is merely a figment of Amit Shah's imagination'. (*India Today* 2020)

The convergence of aphorism, surrealism, and logical thinking—the tukde-tukde gang cannot exist if it has no members; therefore it must be a figment of the imagination—became a mark of interventions by the organic intellectual in this period. Surrealism (or the particular tonality that goes by that name) is often not so much a critique of rationality as a restating of the obvious. Magritte reminds us, for instance, in relation to his portrait of a pipe, through a caption below it, that '*Ceci n'est pas une pipe*' (This is not a pipe). What we call rationality embeds us in convention that prompts us to look at a painting of a pipe and say: 'That's a pipe.' Magritte's caption pre-empts our 'rational' response and reminds us of the angularity, the potentially liberatory, rather than the constraining workings, of logic. This kind of thinking—to do with the stating of the obvious—inflects the Zomato tweet too ('Food doesn't have a religion. It is a religion') and Gopinathan's remark: 'We seem to be perfectly fine with it'—that is, with the suspension of the fundamental rights of a large section of the population. 'I also see in some small ways how I am also a part of it. I think if I had a newspaper, the only thing I would be printing would be "19" on the front page, because today is the nineteenth day.'

The obvious is disorienting, as it is hidden by habits of individual, collective, and institutional thinking; confronted, it can have a surreal—even a spiritual—power. The organic intellectual's method is to find ways of bringing the obvious to our attention through estrangement, rather than necessarily speaking in terms of political affinities, as traditional intellectuals do.

Again, I call Saket Gokhale an organic intellectual because he seems to come from one of the many hidden lineages that form the true mainstream of any country (rather than an elite conception of a mainstream, which works out of power centres). His father was a police inspector in Bombay. He went to Wilson College—a good college, but not one that has a direct conduit to the self-appointed intelligentsia and to scholarships to Oxbridge, as do Delhi colleges like St Stephen's and Jawaharlal Nehru University, and, to a lesser extent, Jadavapur University in Calcutta. He earned a degree in English and then taught English in a school in the Czech Republic. He returned to India and worked in journalism but didn't become well known in a way that he might *transcend* journalism or his non-elite, middle-class background. He remains an organic intellectual by choice and by default, although he has recently joined politics. I don't see him as having entered the transcendent milieu of Gramsci's traditional intellectual, where class and economic provenance and markers are subsumed by the lineage the intellectual claims as their own, and by the professionalised thought they practise. Gokhale's defining context is Indian society.

ON 28TH JANUARY 2020, A COMEDIAN NAMED KUNAL Kamra heckled a well-known (many would say notorious) television anchor, Arnab Goswami, on an IndiGo Airlines flight from Bombay to Lucknow. Goswami is famous for his anti-liberal tirades and the hysteria-inducing manner in which he brings up the transgressions of the 'tukde-tukde gang'. It's a term he has relished using, though he didn't invent it; the coinage is claimed by another TV anchor, Sudhir Chaudhary of Zee News, who said it was aimed at 'designer journalists' and 'English-speaking Page 3 celebrities'. (Deol, Sharma and Jha 2020) 'Page 3', the third page of the city-based supplements of national newspapers, dedicated to pictures of 'famous' people, is a feature of Indian Anglophone broadsheets that has emerged in the time of globalisation and economic deregulation. This is a space that the Gramscian 'traditional intellectual' would have abhorred, but the barrier separating the intellectual, the writer, and the activist from the 'celebrity' is one among many barriers that have vanished with deregulation. Not only have intellectuals, in the last three decades, embraced celebrity and been encouraged to do so, but celebrities have also been allowed to be intellectuals. The second category casually permeates the first, so that we may say today that *only* the celebrity is an intellectual. Even in the case of the thinker, the particularity of their work and the specificity of their critique remain curiously out of sight, while the thinker remains in full view. In literary festivals, the principal attractions advertised as 'writers' are film stars, politicians and sports people. The last three or four years saw lists of 'leading intellectuals' in Indian publications in which serious thinkers were often hard to find. The one crucial quality that the celebrity has in common with the Gramscian 'traditional intellectual' is an apparent transcendence of the economic order: their work and presence aren't defined entirely by class, profession, or the context of the economy—as, say, our jobs are. When Sudhir Chaudhary mentions 'designer journalists' and 'English-speaking Page 3 celebrities', he is referring to celebrities, intellectuals, and this transcendental space.

Kamra, the stand-up comic, went up to Goswami and heckled him repeatedly on the flight, but reportedly apologised to flight staff whenever he was cautioned by them, and returned each time to his seat. As a result of his antics, he was banned from flying on IndiGo for six months; this ban, following tweets from Civil Aviation Minister Hardeep Singh Puri, was widened to include three other airlines. IndiGo later reduced its ban to three months. Rohit Mateti, the flight captain that day, 28th January, sent a letter to IndiGo management soon after the ban, in which he described the events that had taken place on the flight, and concluded:

As Captain of 6E5317 BOM-LKO on 28.01.2020, I do not find the aforementioned events reportable in any way. Mr. Kamra's behaviour while unsavoury, was NOT qualifying of a Level 1 Unruly passenger. Indeed we pilots can all attest to incidents similar and/or worse in nature that were not deemed Unruly... Furthermore, I was disheartened to learn that my Airline has taken action in this case solely on the basis of Social Media posts, with no consultation whatsoever with the Pilot-in-Command. This is somewhat unprecedented in my 9 years of Airline flying. Moving forward, am I to understand that the bar for interpretation of a Disruptive passenger is lower/different when it comes to high profile cases? Perhaps the SEP Manual is to be amended to reflect this? I would like a clarification from the Airline as this leaves a lot of room for ambiguity. (NDTV 2020)

This dependency on the rationality of the system is typical of the organic intellectual. The system represents not so much an order as the guarantee of reasonable parameters, which must also be reasonably interpreted. Responsibility within the system means a constant exercising of rational judgement—exemplified by the flight attendants and the captain himself. Striking, especially, are the questions Mateti raises about the limits of the system that the state (as in the Ministry of Aviation) appropriates and claims to represent: 'Moving forward, am I to understand that the bar for interpretation of a Disruptive passenger is lower/different when it comes to high profile cases? Perhaps the SEP Manual is to be amended to reflect this? I would like a clarification from the Airline as this leaves a lot of room for ambiguity.'

'Perhaps the SEP Manual is to be amended to reflect this?'—here is the same contained humour (different from grievance or outrage) that we've also seen in the responses from Zomato, Gopinathan, and Gokhale. The amended Safety and Emergency Procedures (SEP) manual Mateti proposes—in which 'the bar for interpretation of a Disruptive passenger is lower/different when it comes to high profile cases'—is a Kafkaesque construct, bringing together strangeness and comedy. It is comparable to Gokhale's query: 'What are the names of the members of the "tukde-tukde gang"?' These are essentially logical propositions dealing with truth value.

The 'organic intellectual' was, it seems to me, at this time—early 2020—discovering a language with which to counter the abuse of authority, a language that long seemed to have become unavailable to, say, the 'traditional intellectual' or 'designer journalist'. This may have had to do with their job- and work-defined positions, which did not inhabit a space of transcendence—their access to resources of rationality inherent in the system.

The 'traditional intellectual' had often risked more than they had bargained for in the first term of the BJP/NDA government: prison sentences and neglect in prison in the worst cases; accusations of sedition; censure, harassment, and trolling. The domain of the traditional intellectual was, most commonly, the domain of the custodianship of rights, free speech, democracy, and values exercised by, among other means, letters of protest, letters composed either on behalf of jailed activists or against the abetment of xenophobia, signed by hundreds (including myself) every month or fortnight. It was crucial for this custodianship to exist, to not hand it over entirely to the government. The domain of the organic intellectual was the system itself. Mateti, unlike activists, didn't write to the prime minister; he wrote to his superiors at IndiGo. The traditional intellectual, even in jail, retained their self-definition as activist or intellectual. The organic intellectual risked, at once, their self-definition—say, as pilot or businessman—and livelihood. Their argumentation, consequently, comprised an unexpected challenge.

IN DECEMBER 2019, I TOOK PART IN A LONG ANTI-CAA march from Central Calcutta to the Gandhi statue near Chowringhee a mile south. The march differed from one I had taken part in in 2013 to protest the Bengal Chief Minister Mamata Banerjee's high-handed behaviour during her visit to a village called Kamduni, where a student named Shipra Ghosh had been gang-raped and murdered. It had seemed important, then, to stand against the chief minister's autocratic tendencies, which responded to any questioning of herself as a questioning of the validity of governance itself—it was important to be able to speak up without fear. This was a year before the BJP's arrival at the political centre, and six years prior to their second term, when fear would be elevated by the BJP to the dominant ethos, and Banerjee too would find herself increasingly hemmed in not by journalists and public criticism but by the state itself. In seven years (2014–20), she would be forced to reconsider, given the BJP's Constitution-dismantling proclivities, her own investment in democracy and free speech.

That 2013 procession I joined was thick with the presence of the traditional intellectual type—activists, academics, writers, filmmakers. There was some wryly expressed nervousness of course: the political scientist Partha Chatterjee noted to me that each of us was being watched and would be added to a 'list'. The looks we got from people on the sidewalk—the traders, vendors, and people who lived and worked in the areas along Central Avenue, down which we were walking—were sceptical, uninterested, or slightly mocking. They were, of course, fed up by then with the chronic protest marches under the Left Front government that had been in power in West Bengal for thirty-four years until 2011: events that were rustled up periodically by, paradoxically, the then ruling party. But the gaze also carried the coldness that the daily-wage earner and blue- and white-collar worker alike felt against the 'traditional intellectual'—a constituency, identifiable from the juxtaposition of certain classless class markers (kurtas, beards, jeans, glasses), that was *expected* to protest. This coldness, in other cities, especially Delhi, then turned, from 2014 onwards, into tacit but palpable support for attacks made by the NDA/BJP government against institutions like the Jawaharlal Nehru University.

The December 2019 march felt different because—although activists and academics did participate in it—its demography was dominated by 'ordinary' people who were defined more by the work they did than by their politics. The number of Muslims in the march—the largest I have witnessed or been part of—exceeded the number of Hindus, but Hindus took part too. These were mainly people who lived or worked in the areas around Central

Avenue, Dalhousie Square, and Chowringhee. The march was not only part of the anti-CAA protests then taking place without—as I have said before—any apparent political leadership across the country; it also came not long after the brutal police response in Delhi to the anti-CAA protests in Jamia Millia Islamia University and then at JNU and Aligarh Muslim University. Near the Gandhi statue, where the long procession ended, speeches were made by the activist Harsh Mander, who had helped organise the march, and students from Jamia Millia who had come in from Delhi.

The other difference, for me, was the gaze of the onlookers: the vendors and pedestrians on the arcade by the Grand Hotel, cutting across Lindsay Street, which leads to New Market. I was struck by the absorption and absence of hostility in the stares. It was as if they had grasped instinctively, even before the protesters had, that what was happening before them was not political in the usual sense of being party political; a new politics was being made here, albeit under duress. The historian and JNU professor Tanika Sarkar's words in an interview at the time with the *Anandabazar Patrika* came back to me as I walked. (*Anandabazar Patrika* 2020) Sarkar discussed the protestors' treatment at the hands of the police in Delhi after the Jamia violence on 18th December: they were treated respectfully, perhaps because of their class, education, and age, but also gathered into vans and dropped off late at night at some nameless location outside Delhi, from where they made their way back on foot and by bus. Unlike me, Sarkar is a veteran of the protest rally, and the observation she'd made that returned to me now was this: 'ordinary' people, who generally regard protestors with contempt, were empathetic on this occasion in December 2019.

The traditional intellectual was greatly outnumbered in the Calcutta march by the sort of person who usually plays the onlooker's role. This may have had partly to do with the fact that fewer intellectuals wanted to be openly associated—given the multiplicity of retributive measures—with protest in the BJP's second term. But it was also partly to do with the energised mass involvement in those months, an involvement that had arrived at a compact with the traditional intellectual, as was evident from the appreciative responses to the speeches given in front of the Gandhi statue by writer-activist Harsh Mander and others. On these occasions, we saw the rise of the organic intellectual, who had no markers or delineating features, so to speak, but both formed the crowd and sometimes stood out from it. I have in mind, for instance, the shy man who stood midstream in the procession under the Chowringhee flyover with a sign demanding: Bure din wapas karo (Give us back the bad times).

Here was an example of wordplay expressing a logic that countered the ruling party's own assertions, specifically the slogan 'Achhe din aane wale hain' (Good times are going to come), coined by Narendra Modi for the 2014 elections, in a way that a marshalling of figures couldn't. 'Bure din wapas karo' was a rebuttal of Modi's promise; a reminder that it becomes beholden upon the 'bad' sometimes to vanquish the 'good'.

ON 14TH JANUARY 2020, MY WIFE AND I VISITED THE Park Circus protests in Calcutta, which, like the one in Shaheen Bagh, Delhi, were arranged and dominated by Muslim women, most of them in traditional burqa. Large posters of Gandhi, Subhas Chandra Bose, and B.R. Ambedkar, as well as a plethora of Indian flags, surrounded us. This was happening across the country: the appropriation and reinvigoration of national symbols (some of them, like the flag, commonly claimed by political parties or patriots; others, like Ambedkar, seen as the icons of certain groups or communities, like the Dalits or the 'left-liberal' intellectuals) by a mainstream of men and women transformed by, and contributing to, the anti-CAA protests, including, of course, much of the Muslim population.

In the process, the flag changed from being the empty symbol it had been under Congress rule, waved during Republic Day parades, or the instrument of intimidation it had become under the BJP—when you could be beaten up if you didn't stand up for the national anthem or vociferously echo the cry Bharat Mata ki Jai! The national flag became a sign promising a number of new meanings.

Similarly, Ambedkar, it seemed to me, was being reinserted—both as the face of a historically oppressed group, the Dalits, and as a drafter of the Constitution—into the national consciousness far more persuasively than various seminar discussions in the last decade had managed to do. The traditional intellectual's attempts to bring Ambedkar into the discussion as part of a critique of the blindness to caste hadn't foreseen the extent to which he could be invoked, universally, in the context of democratic rights. And the role that the Indian flag could play in protest had not been previously imagined. To lift symbols (the Constitution, a picture of Ambedkar, the national flag) and bring them together with the features of various other realities (religion, the burqa) was to make an argument, to create a new case for reimagining the human and the political. The connections these juxtapositions asked us to make—between posters, flags, and women making speeches, or cheering, or distributing tea and biscuits—involved reusing our powers of reasoning rather than tapping into a readymade vocabulary of dissent.

As we entered the Park Circus maidan, we saw a young woman in a burqa at the microphone (speaker after speaker, mostly women, would follow) raising slogans. Then she began to speak in Urdu/Hindi, pointing out the privileges she had as an 'educated' woman, which, she said, was why she was standing before the microphone: she was aware of her rights, her haq. 'Some of us may be students here, some of us may be children, but none of us are stupid.' Indeed, there were children present—high-spirited, but certainly not bewakoof: stupid or gullible. After chanting a few more slogans, the young woman said: 'The name of Gandhi came up earlier, but I confess I was never a wholehearted follower of the Gandhian way. I'm an admirer of Subhas Chandra Bose.' There was applause. 'But now, when I see how our students are being beaten up, I feel great pride and begin to understand the value and fruits of ahimsa [non-violence].' She raised slogans for the students of JNU, Jamia and AMU; the crowd joined in. The man standing next to me said: 'She's my wife.'

I liked that she'd presented the arc of her thought to us: that Gandhi's appeal to her had been a qualified one until she had realised, in the last month, the purpose of ahimsa. This was in keeping with the various throwaway remarks made by organic intellectuals from July 2010 onwards: that there were no readymade resources for political protest if protest was not to become a repetition of pieties, that reasoning needed to be enlisted and put to work.

We, too, began to participate in protest as a form of logical thinking: a reconsideration of the language and uses of nationalism, that took nothing for granted, neither an inherited iconography nor the presence of children in a gathering. For my part, I inferred that deep religiosity—of which the burqa was a sign—was not incompatible with being deeply invested in the secular. In fact, it seemed possible that 'secularism' had always been impelled and renovated by the wisdom that is made available to people through religious inheritances. The space of religion and the space of the secular state weren't distinguished by a demarcation in Park Circus, as in the European idea of the secular. The secular state didn't just accommodate various religions, as in the Indian conception of secularism. Religion didn't mean opposing the secular or delegitimising it as 'pseudo-secular', which was the BJP's model. The religious was an indispensable component of the secular.

———

IN WHAT WAY DID INDIA'S RELIGIOUS INHERITANCE energise the protests against xenophobia, in that it generated fresh meaning rather than remain centred on a fight for religious equality? In what way did members of the majority who contributed substantially to the protests also reshape them through resources available to them from a long religious inheritance? I suggest they did this by having recourse to a tradition of rationality within religion, expressed over millennia through philosophical tracts, songs, and poems. The matter of equal rights in connection with the practice of religion is not really a religious preoccupation; it's a constitutional one. Religious preoccupations in India are often polysemic, to do with meaning and arriving at clarity of thought. It is within this tradition that the protests need to be located, too. Xenophobia wasn't fought, in the anti-CAA protests, through the historic 'syncretism'—an old cliché of seminar rooms—attributed to religions in India. It was fought through religion's historic access, in this country, to rationality.

One evening in 2016, my family and I were watching, against better judgement, a Bengali-language news channel, one among an array whose hallucinatory atmosphere makes tabloid journalism seem balanced. After ten minutes, I said, 'We never watch this channel. Let's not start now.' Instinctively, I went to another channel we no longer watch either—the government national outlet, Doordarshan (literally, 'distant vision'), which had been made largely obsolete in the 1990s with the advent of satellite TV and become synonymous with boredom. That may have been why I went to it: to be out of sync and far away from the tone of the contemporary. What was airing at that moment on Doordarshan was, in a sense, true to its ethos: an interview with the Dalai Lama. I switched off inwardly, but it was good to see him, as perennially cheerful as a family elder. I have categorised the Dalai Lama in my subconscious as a hybrid of family elder and world ambassador, and have suffered and been happy with him without ever feeling I needed to listen to what he said. His words, at that moment, spoke directly to me, given the sort of 'news' we had just been exposed to on the Bengali channel, and I returned to them later: 'Reason can never be defeated by the irrational. Reason is based on pramana [proof or evidence]. In the end, reason is always victorious.'

Until that moment, I had missed the fact that rationality was a crucial ground for religious thought. By religious thought I had (because it was the Dalai Lama who was speaking) Buddhism in mind, and—in a quick retrospective reassessment of what I knew—also Upanishadic poetic-philosophical texts, the Gita, the Jataka tales, Sufism (with its privileging of direct contact, which is a variation of pramana, over mediation and second-hand interpretations), and the songs of the Bhakti movement. It seemed like an extraordinary error, suddenly, to have identified the history of reason, or reasoning, with the West and/or with science, and to have proceeded to either celebrate or critique it on that basis. Those who either castigated or acknowledged the value of certain cultural manifestations, formations, lineages, or movements—say, religion, or the non-West, or romanticism—did so often largely on the assumption that their main drawback or appeal was that they were anti- or non-rational. This was how this debate, worn out by now, was cast, and its terms still pervade our thinking, so that if we speak up for, say, religion, we do so to remind ourselves of the significance of what can't be accessed through rationality. The Dalai Lama's observation set a chain of associations into motion in my head, and made me realise that rationality has a history that is much older and a meaning that's richer than the ones we take as givens from the situations in which we place them. Religion's refinement and honing of rationality are incisive, and have been essential, historically, to dissent.

What does religion use reason against? Post-Enlightenment convention, which we have internalised, states that religion's enemy *is*, in fact, science and reason, and vice versa. A more careful examination reveals that rationality, in India, is religious thought's means of refuting hegemony, and hegemony, until 300 years ago, in India as elsewhere, was religion. (The narrative of Christianity and its wars with the state and science have to be distinguished from the argumentation I'm referring to.) So religion uses reason to refute religion, or, more precisely, bogus religion—from which (in case we need reminding) xenophobia mainly emanates. Here's an example from the fifteenth-century Bhakti poet Kabir, the son of Muslim weavers, deploying logic against the habit of equating religiosity with *signs* of religiosity:

> If going naked
> Brought liberation,
> The deer of the forest
> Would attain it first.

> If a shaven head
> Was a sign of piety,
> Ewes would be
> Pious too.
>
> If holding back the semen
> Brought you closer to heaven,
> A steer would
> Lead the way.

The song ends:

> There's no salvation
> Without Rama, says Kabir.
> Not to know it
> Is really dumb.

Some premises are being examined here and being tested against another premise at the end. The propositions in question have to do with whether the markers of renunciation, asceticism, and piety (an unclothed body, a shaven head, holding in semen) are a guarantee of spiritual attainment. If they were,

'Ewes would be / Pious too.' The benchmark is not the observance of a form of practice, but direct experience: 'no salvation / Without Rama.' 'Rama,' here, is proof (pramana); the accessories presented as evidence of spirituality are accoutrements that are easily acquired—in the case of the deer and the ewe, acquired without any effort at all.

The translator Mehrotra's note to the Kabir poem says:

> John Stratton Hawley and Mark Jurgensmeyer, who have translated this poem in *Songs of the Saints of India* (1988), say in a note, 'The practices of wandering naked, shaving the head, and learning to retain the semen all pertain to yoga in some form' … The first two stanzas of the poem are almost identical with those by Saraha, written half a millennium earlier: 'if going naked means release / then the dog and the jackal / must have it; / / if baldness is perfection / then a young girl's bottom / must have it'.

This reliance on logic in devotion (where the rational mind is indistinguishable from the devotee's mind) had been going on for some time before this was composed. We might look back to the Gita, which warns its readers that studying the Vedas is not itself a guarantee of salvation; and to the Buddha, who explores and then rejects extreme physical austerity as a route to enlightenment. In the instances I've cited above, a logical proposition is completed on the basis of the weighing of evidence (pramana). This process rejects conventions to do with the sacrosanct; reason vouches for the importance of complete surrender, but it is crucial for it to not metamorphose into non-rationality itself, to continue to use reasoning to negotiate the path through the overtly or bogusly religious to the divine.

Here is another verse by Kabir, which again comprises a testing of propositions for their inherent absurdity:

> O pundit, your hairsplitting's
> So much bullshit. I'm surprised
> You still get away with it.
>
> If parroting the name
> Of Rama brought salvation

> Then saying *sugarcane*
> Should sweeten the mouth,
> Saying *fire* burn the feet,
> Saying *water* slake thirst...

Again, logic and rationality are put to the service of the truth of religious experience. Kabir's words speak to the way bhakts (literally, 'devotees', but today referring to right-wing vigilantes) cry Jai Shri Ram (victory to Lord Rama) and Bharat Mata ki Jai, and also extort these cries from others. Crazed violence can't be stopped with violence, but increasingly during the anti-CAA protests people began to tap into a language of rationality.

The Dalai Lama's mention of pramana took me back to a song by the Baul Lalon Fakir that I had first heard as a child and then in a recording by the singer Amar Pal as a teenager. (The Bengali equivalent of the word here is 'proman'.)

> Shob loke koy
> Lalon ki jaat ei shongshare

Lalon koy jaater ki rup
Dekhlam na ei nojore

Bamun chini poita proman
Bamni chini kishe re

Keo mala keo toshbi gole
Tai to ki jaat bhinno bole
Jawa kimba ashar kale
Jaater chinho roy kishe

These are the song's first three verses in the version I heard by Amar Pal. Lalon is said to have lived for more than a hundred years, from the late eighteenth to the late nineteenth century, and the Baul movement he was a part of is a Vaishnav (that is, related to the cult of Krishna) offshoot in Bengal of the Bhakti movement. 'Baul' may mean 'crazy' or 'mad', related to the Braj word 'bawra', where madness has to do with the love of God, the sort of obstreperous love that makes you an outcast. As with Kabir, it isn't certain if Lalon was Hindu or Muslim. 'Crazy' though his kind may be, Lalon relies on a tradition of rationality when it comes to discarding all-consuming but essentially bogus religious questions. In the first verse, he says (the translation is mine): 'Everyone asks / What religion does Lalon follow in this world? / Lalon says, I still haven't seen / The shape or form of religion with my eyes / If a sacred thread's proof that a man's a Brahmin / How would you identify a Brahmin woman?' On the one hand, Lalon reminds us of the fact that what isn't visible to the eye can't exist: religion has no material form in the way an object has. On the other, the sacred thread is proof (proman) of the Brahmin's caste; problematically then, a Brahmin woman has nothing to mark her out as Brahmin. Lalon is sifting through the matter of proman in the song, examining the way its lack can be telling and reminding his audience that, in certain instances, what seems like proof (the sacred thread) is really a sign of legitimacy.

'Some wear garlands, some rosaries,' the third verse goes, 'And in that way they distinguish their religion from the other's / But at the moment of departure or arrival / What are the signs of one's religion?'

Logic and reasoning aren't directed in this tradition (in contrast to the post-Enlightenment Europe of science and reason) towards invalidating God's existence, though, if they were, the grounds for doing so would be identical to the grounds on which Lalon's song questions the existence of religion: both religion and God are concepts that lack material form and are therefore unverifiable. But in Indian argumentation against the false or irrational, the matter of God's validity is, in the Buddha's terminology, 'irrelevant'. The poet Arun Koltakar, famous for *Jejuri*, the poem-sequence he wrote about visiting the eponymous pilgrimage town, echoed this position when he was asked by an interviewer if he believed in God: 'I leave the question alone. I don't think I have to take a position about God one way or the other.' (Mehrotra 1992)

To Indian reasoning, whether the object of adoration, devotion, or focus exists is a secondary or non-question; what's scrutinised is whether the adoration or focus is real and self-forgetful, or self-interested and factitious: 'If parroting the name / Of Rama brought salvation / Then saying *sugarcane* / Should sweeten the mouth.' This form of argumentation and thinking goes back to the sixth century BCE to the philosophical tradition of nyaya, or logic (in today's Hindi, 'nyaya' simply means 'law'), which differs from logic in the European sense in that its concerns are epistemological: it examines types of pramana to enquire into the provenances of forms of knowledge. European logic has remained, for most of its history, an *instrument* of the logos, or knowledge, from which it derives its name, not an enquiry into it; nyaya and its related form of enquiry, Buddhist logic, are a scrutiny of logos (as in the Gita's throwaway caveat about the study of the Vedas being no guarantee of illumination). All of this—Kabir, Lalon, Sufis, Bhakti, Buddhism, nyaya—create a history and context of rationality that begin to be accessed, I think, by the organic intellectual and expressed in statements like: 'Food doesn't have a religion. It is a religion'; or 'the "tukde-tukde gang" does not officially exist & is merely a figment of Amit Shah's imagination'; or 'Moving forward, am I to understand that the bar for interpretation of a Disruptive passenger is lower/different when it comes to high profile cases? Perhaps the SEP Manual is to be amended to reflect this?'

By the time of the introduction of the CAA, bogus religiosity or bogus nationalism could no longer be addressed by the conventions of humanism, liberalism, or pluralism; they had to be rebutted by a form of reasoning that had entered the atmosphere two millennia ago and then, in the last millennium, had become disseminated through mass movements and their songs and poetry. These forms of reasoning were, I think, more available to the blue- and white-collar worker than to an intelligentsia that transcended the system; these traditions of rationality, of argumentation—in Sanskrit, tarka; in Pali, takka—have run in and out through the system in a way academia and institutions of knowledge don't recognise. The CAA could not be countered, in the end, by a single leader, like Gandhi, or a single idea, like ahimsa. Amit Shah's words and their chilling elisions *had* to be met by rationality, and a rationality whose history, resources, and tonalities in India were less narrow than in the West, and were a feature of, rather than in opposition to, the quest for a truly religious life. Amartya Sen wrote about the Indian's 'argumentative' traditions, mainly to demonstrate that our liberal understanding of 'democratic debate' had a very old lineage in India. (Sen 2005) But, in the utterances of the organic intellectuals and in the anti-CAA demonstrations, what I encountered was an unprecedented mobilisation by people of a historical discourse of reasoning that revivified liberal democracy, but whose origins liberals didn't fully understand, although some among them (see Tanika Sarkar's interview) sensed something 'new' at work.

Among its resources, besides songs and poems, were jokes and paradoxes (Bure din wapas karo; 'Give us back the bad times'). Humour as reasoning goes as far back as the tales of the Jatakas and, in the last millennium, to the extraordinary seventh-century rock carvings or frieze in Mahabalipuram often called 'Arjuna's penance', where Arjuna, hero of the Mahabharata, is one among many figures created from a rockface: he is standing on one leg, performing yogic austerities, and (in the most startling such instance in sculpture) his stomach has caved in. Not far from him is a cat in a similar posture, smirking, imitating the pose of saintliness, but (in another marvel of sculpture) its stomach is softly distended. Here is rationality, humour, and critique, where what's at stake is not God but the nature of true devotion: be careful of the fat cat, no matter how fiercely he espouses religion. This is not satire as we have come to understand it via Europe. The fat cat is not simply parodying Arjuna, nor is the sculptor just exposing the cat as a fraud. The cat is as *necessary* an element in the frieze as Arjuna is; the frieze can't be reduced to the terms of narrative or satire because it's a cosmology—as I now feel the anti-CAA movement was, with its posters of the founding fathers, its deliberate brandishing of the national flag, its burqa-clad women, the accompanying children: a sudden public quest to understand our place in the universe.

Fascism is a form, or deliberate manipulation, of irrationality (powerfully expressed through race-worship and xenophobia). Thomas Mann, noting the rise of National Socialism, gave a public lecture in Berlin on 17th October 1930, called 'Deutsche Ansprache' (an Address to Germans), with the subtitle 'Ein Apell an die Vernunft' (an Appeal to Reason). Yet reason, as I have pointed out, has a very clearly demarcated—a limited—history in Europe, separated firmly from religion, and, by implication, in the West, from the masses. The predominance of rationality following the Enlightenment is coterminous with the predominance from then on of man over God. In contrast, the Urdu term 'insaniyat' (humanity—that is, humanity as a quality rather than as a term to denote, collectively, human beings), which was rediscovered and invoked repeatedly during the protests, suggested no such supplanting. Insaniyat is not incompatible with the adoration of God in the way 'humanism' is. These registers of meaning were crucial to widening the political impact and power of the protests. Mann himself was, of course, limited in 1930 by being a writer and, therefore, a figure who transcended class—the process through which this transcendence takes place in bourgeois society is explored with great acuity in his own fiction, beginning with the early

Tonio Kröger. His 'appeal to reason' would thereby have limited itself.

The one modern Anglophone intellectual counterpart to the kind of rationality I'm discussing was, in the late nineteenth century, literary criticism, whose task for Matthew Arnold is not only to determine the nature of the valuable but also to reject false markers of literary value. (His term for this pursuit in the 1880 essay 'The Study of Poetry', now embarrassing to us, is 'high seriousness'.) The bogus or instrumental forms of 'creative' practice, legitimised by commonly recognised markers, have to be countered by a form of reasoning called 'criticism'. What *is* valuable can't be ascertained except through direct contact: for Arnold, this involves the method, gauche and lordly at once, of simply presenting us with quotations from those he considers 'great' poets. 'Everything depends on the reality of a poet's classic character. If he is a dubious classic, let us sift him; if he is a false classic, let us explode him,' he says. And a critique is articulated in the essay against what had become, in Arnold's time, the conventional mode of reasoning in determining value: the philological-historical method in ascertaining what a classic is.

> The elaborate philological groundwork which we require them to lay is in theory an admirable preparation for appreciating the Greek and Latin authors worthily. The more thoroughly we lay the groundwork, the better we shall be able, it may be said, to enjoy the authors. True, if time were not so short, and schoolboys' wits not so soon tired and their power of attention exhausted; only, as it is, the elaborate philological preparation goes on, but the authors are little known and less enjoyed. So with the investigator of 'historic origins' in poetry. He ought to enjoy the true classic all the better for his investigations; he often is distracted from the enjoyment of the best, and with the less good he overbusies himself, and is prone to over-rate it in proportion to the trouble which it has cost him.

The pandit, the Brahmin, is being shown up here; a special discourse of reasoning is being fashioned, whose yardstick is not the verifiable, but 'enjoyment'. We must keep in mind that Arnold had been studying the Gita for decades, and recall, too, since these contiguities posit themselves, Kabir's intolerance of the 'dubious classic'. Literary criticism, by the late nineteenth century, in Tagore as in Arnold, becomes a new form of reasoning that can't be accounted for by the Enlightenment. It is no accident that its Anglophone turn occurs at a time when philosophical-religious texts from beyond (in Raymond Schwab's words) 'the humanism of the Mediterranean basin' (Said 1978, 77) are circulating in Europe.

This may seem like a digression, but it is an attempt to acknowledge the various experiences of value and reasoning that might renovate the political, or whose historicity, power, and place in the world might be grasped anew through some present-day political event.

ONE OF THE EMOTIONS BROUGHT BACK TO US BY the songs and poems that unified the anti-CAA protesters across the country was the humane melancholy of nationalism, its poetic ambiguity.

Nationalist exhortations like Jai Hind, first used during the struggle for independence, had been made unidimensional and minatory under the NDA government. The national anthem, sung in free India with hope and uncertainty, now demanded mandatory obeisance and implied a threat of punishment. The genre of national songs, created in India in the late nineteenth and early twentieth centuries as an expression of faith in the possibility of the impossible, had lost their capacity to move under the BJP as nationalism became wholly triumphalist. One of the revisionary achievements of the protests was to give that capacity back to songs, such as Faiz Ahmed Faiz's 'Hum Dekhenge' (We Shall See) and D.L. Roy's 'Dhana Dhanyo Pushpe Bhara' (Full of Riches, Abundance and Flowers).

What is it that makes triumphal assertions in poetry moving, causing us at times to weep? It's not a feeling of unalloyed victory. Praise in poetry and song is an act of love, and love involves vulnerability. What or whom we love—beloved or nation—we find vulnerable, and we praise not only to celebrate but also to protect. Our love makes *us* vulnerable too: the person who praises is not characterised by assertiveness, except in an overt, rhetorical sense. The undercurrent of homage and love is not irony but melancholy, and this is why we are moved, rather than emboldened, when we hear the chorus in Sophocles's *Antigone* observe:

> Wonders are many, and none is more wonderful than man; the power that crosses the white sea, driven by the stormy south-wind, making a path under surges that threaten to engulf him; and Earth, the eldest of the gods, the immortal, the unwearied, doth he wear, turning the soil with the offspring of horses, as the ploughs go to and fro from year to year.

Poetry expresses tonalities of wishfulness while seeming to affirm fulfilment, because it knows it is the former rather than the latter that comprises human grandeur. The critic Michel Chaouli pointed out in a talk he gave in a symposium called 'On Failing' in 2020 at Ashoka University in Delhi (https://www.youtube.com/watch?v=iGjgOcC0K5Q&t=15s) that this quality of vulnerability inflects the German idealist Johann

Gottlieb Fichte's confirmation of man's singularity in *Grundlage des Naturrechts nach Prinzipien der Wissenschaftslehre* (Fichte [1796] 1966, 382):

> It has been asked if the human being was destined to walk on four feet or upright. I think he is not destined for either of these. It has been left to him, as a species, to choose for himself his mode of locomotion. A human body can walk on four feet; people have been found who have been raised among animals and who can do this with incredible swiftness. In my view the species has freely raised itself off the ground and thereby acquired the capacity to cast its gaze around itself, allowing it to take in half the universe in the sky, while the eye of the animal, because of its position, is bound to the ground, which carries its nourishment. By raising itself up, it [the human species] has gained two tools of freedom from nature: the two arms, which, free of all animal tasks, dangle from the body, awaiting the command of the will, formed entirely to be fit for the purposes of this will. Thanks to its daring gait, which is a continuous expression of its boldness and its skill in observing its balance, it keeps

practicing its freedom and its reason, remains in a state of becoming and expresses it. Thanks to this posture it moves its life into the realm of light and keeps fleeing the earth, which it touches with the part of itself that is as small as possible. For the animal, the ground is bed and table; the human being raises all that above the earth. (Translated by Michel Chaouli)

Here, the terms Fichte (1762–1814) uses look back to Sophocles, but also possess the newfound ebullience of human-centred Enlightenment thinking. Yet something is happening to the language, especially after 'Thanks to its daring gait', in phrases like 'remains in a state of becoming' and 'moves its life into the realm of life and keeps fleeing the earth' that exceeds volition, mastery and will, and inadvertently, and movingly, lapses into the language of contingency: man is not entirely aware of how he became man and what the meaning of that becoming entails. These delicate, contradictory tonalities are destroyed by imperialism, racism, historicism (that is, the idea of progress), and the nationalist state.

Students at the Indian Institute of Technology (IIT) in Kanpur sang Faiz Ahmed Faiz's 'Hum Dekhenge' in protest and in solidarity with students at Jamia Millia and Jawaharlal Nehru Universities in New Delhi on 17th December 2019 (two days after the police attacks). A member of the IIT Kanpur faculty, Dr Vashi Mant Sharma, registered a complaint against the protest, saying two lines in particular had hurt his 'religious sentiments': *'Jab arz-e-Khuda ke Ka'abe se, sab buth uthwaae jaayenge / Hum ahl-e-safa mardood-e-haram, masnad pe bithaaye jaayenge / Sab taaj uchhaale jaayenge, sab takht giraaye jaayenge'* ('From the abode of God, when the icons of falsehood will be removed / When we, the faithful, who have been barred from sacred places, will be seated on a high pedestal / When crowns will be tossed, when thrones will be brought down') (The Wire 2020). Sharma saw this as an allegorical reference to the Mughal invasion of India, which was accompanied by the destruction of idols and temples—the word 'buth', meaning 'idol' or 'figure', plays into this interpretation. The fact that Faiz

(1911–84) was Pakistani couldn't have helped, although he'd been a Marxist and an atheist, and his song had been composed to dissent against General Zia-ul-Haq's Islamicising regime in Pakistan. As a result of Sharma's complaint, a committee was put in place at IIT Kanpur, and six students and five teachers were 'counselled'—which must mean 'warned'—for their role in the protest.

Here's my admittedly cursory attempt to translate the words:

> We shall see—
> It's certain we too shall see
> The day that was promised to us
> And set indelibly in iron
>
> When the boulder-weight of tyranny
> Will scatter like wisps of cotton
> And under the feet of the reigned-over
> The earth will pound like a heart beating
> And over the heads of those who govern
> Lightning will burn and crackle

When all idols will be vacated
From the holy places
And we, the dispossessed and displaced,
Will be returned to our inheritance,
Each crown will be flung away,
Each seat of power brought down

Allah's name will remain: nothing more—
He, who is present and absent too,
He, who is both scene and spectator;
The cry 'I am truth' will be heard,
The cry that is me as it is you,
And everywhere will reign God's progeny
Which is what I am, as you are.

We are moved by this in a way that we aren't by actionable words. There is an ambiguity of emotion here to do with the phrase 'we shall see', which is inflected with both defiance and defeat (the victorious don't say 'we shall see'); and Allah, who, we are told the moment we are promised the prospect of his ubiquity, is both 'present and absent' (hazir hai aur gayab bhi), pointing to the curious sense of annulment we experience in ourselves in the midst of the song's prescience of plenitude. Like love, protest implies surrender: a surrender of the personal, in the course of which what is 'present and absent' in ourselves converge. This convergence, in turn, leads to, instead of unequivocal triumph, a melancholy in protest, a melancholy that doesn't paralyse but enables, as this song did for so many in 2020.

The literalism of nationalism allows neither that melancholy nor the contradictory tonality in which it subsists. Neither, to be fair, does the liberal consciousness, which sees the protest poem or song as a *vehicle* for protest rather than a complex experience that exists in and through the texture of poetic language. On 7th January, Riyaz Khan, on the *Times of India* readers' blog, identified himself as an 'Urdu poetry lover' and said he was distressed by the way 'Hum Dekhenge' had been misread. 'People who are cognizant of the art and nuances of poetry know that in poetry words are not used to stress their literal meaning,' he wrote. (Khan 2020) This is a truism of literary criticism and, in the context of the time, a reasonable statement: criticism as an expression of a rationality related to love, the love of 'Urdu poetry', which itself is not unrelated to a wider understanding of democracy, free speech, and insaniyat. The first two sentences of Riyaz Khan's biographical note on the blog page describe him as 'basically a mechanical engineer with MBA in International Business. Currently he is director in an Engineering Services & IT headquartered company in Hyderabad.' In keeping with the time of the anti-CAA protests, Khan seems to have been an organic intellectual who emerged from and made his intervention within the system.

BY THE END OF MARCH 2020, THE PANDEMIC had begun to make its appearance. It gave the government a chance to curtail, and then put an end to, the Shaheen Bagh and Park Circus gatherings. The first lockdown and culpable levels of government mismanagement—precipitating the mass migrations on foot by daily-wage earners—seemed to disperse, with finality, the political movements of early 2020. The government pursued its own agendas of making over national history—the Central Vista project in New Delhi, for instance—just out of sight of the public eye. But the National Register of Citizens, which had an unintendedly devastating and farcical outcome in Assam, in that the majority of people without proper papers turned out to be Hindu, and the CAA seemed to have been temporarily run into the ground. The one political movement that, through tenacity and backing, did succeed during the pandemic was the farmers' movement—the three laws they were protesting against were later repealed.

The anti-CAA protests are testament to the possibility not just of an aim being realised, but also of a universal transformation, and a putting to use of the country's long history of thought for the purposes of democracy in a way not seen even during the freedom movement. It happened—and it now gives us the opportunity to realign how we live and what we know.

REFERENCES

Anandabazar Patrika. 2020. Jan. 3. https://www.anandabazar.com/editorial/interview-of-historian-tanika-sarkar-on-the-running-movement-against-caa-and-nrc-1.1090254.

Deol, Taran, Unnati Sharma, and Fiza Jha. 2020. *The Print.in*, Jan. 22. https://theprint.in/plugged-in/sudhir-chaudhury-boasts-zee-created-tukde-tukde-gang-nidhi-razdan-grills-pavan-verma/352989/.

Fichte, Johann Gottlieb. [1796] *Grundlage des Naturrechts nach Principien der Wissenschaftslehre.* In Fichte, J.G. 1966. Gesamtausgabe I/3. Eds. Reinhard Lauth and Hans Jacob (Stuttgart – Bad Cannstatt: Formmann-Holzboog, 1966), 382.

Hindustan Times. 2020. "'Give us an Undertaking": Man who cancelled Zomato order gets police notice,' June 8. https://www.hindustantimes.com/india-news/give-us-an-undertaking-man-who-cancelled-zomato-order-gets-police-notice/story-ITNSMWk8G5x62HnTVI5KDP.html.

India Today. 2020. "'Have no information on Tukde Tukde Gang": Home ministry in RTI reply,' Jan. 20.

https://www.indiatoday.in/india/story/have-no-information-on-tukde-tukde-gang-home-ministry-in-rti-reply-1638593-2020-01-20.

Kabir. 2011. *Songs of Kabir*, trans. Arvind Krishna Mehrotra. New York: New York Review Books, 23.

Khan, Riyaz. 2020. 'What Firaq Would Have Told Faiz's Critics: "Folks, Don't Murder Poetry"', *Times of India* Readers' Blog, Jan. 7: https://timesofindia.indiatimes.com/readersblog/poor-working-conditions-in-places-relating-to-women/what-firaq-would-have-told-faizs-critics-folks-dont-murder-poetry-9597/.

Kolatkar, Arun. 2005. Jejuri. New York: New York Review Books.

Mehrotra, Arvind Krishna, ed. 1992. *The Oxford India Anthology of Twelve Modern Indian Poets*. New Delhi: Oxford U. Press, 54.

NDTV.com. 2020. Jan. 30. 'Full text of letter.' https://www.ndtv.com/india-news/kunal-kamra-letter-full-text-of-letter-by-pilot-rohit-mateti-who-flew-comedian-kunal-kamra-2172294.

Praveen, S.R. 2019. 'IAS officer Kannan Gopinathan resigns over "lack of freedom of expression".' *The Hindu*, Aug. 24. https://www.thehindu.com/news/national/ias-officer-kannan-gopinathan-resigns-over-lack-of-freedom-of-expression/article29244029.ece.

Ramos, Valeriano, Jr. 1982. *Theoretical Review* No. 27, March–April.

Said, Edward. 1978. *Orientalism*. London: Penguin, 77.

Sen, Amartya. 2005. *The Argumentative Indian*. London: Penguin.

Times of India. 2019. 'Customer wanted a "Hindu food delivery boy", what Zomato founder said,' Debasish Sarkar, July 31. https://timesofindia.indiatimes.com/gadgets-news/customer-wanted-a-hindu-food-delivery-boy-what-zomato-founder-said/articleshow/70461928.cms.

Trilling, Lionel, and Harald Bloom, eds. 1973. *The Oxford Anthology of English Literature: Victorian Poetry and Prose*. London: Oxford U. Press, 237.

TheWire.in. 2020. 'IIT Kanpur Panel Says Reciting Faiz's "Hum Dekhenge" Was "Unsuitable to Time, Place",' Wire staff, March 16. https://thewire.in/rights/faiz-ahmad-faiz-iit-kanpur-hum-dekhenge.

Acknowledgements

This is a revised version of a talk delivered semi-extempore from notes at Jamia Millia Islamia University, New Delhi, on 4th March 2020, as the thirteenth Ahmad Ali Memorial Lecture. It was first published in *Social Research: An International Quarterly*, Volume 88, Number 4, Winter 2021. The text remains more or less identical to the previously published version, and, like the lecture, belongs to a particular moment and context.

On Being Indian was to appear as a Westland publication, but both the publisher and the author/series editor agreed that it was the kind of work that was a natural fit in the Literary Activism series: the series and the work would, hopefully, energise each other. Unlike the other books in the series, it is published independently of the funding support agreement between Ashoka University and Westland Books.

OTHER TITLES IN THE LITERARY ACTIVISM SERIES

Book of Rahim & Other Poems by Arvind Krishna Mehrotra

www.ingramcontent.com/pod-product-compliance
Lightning Source LLC
LaVergne TN
LVHW050031090526
838199LV00126B/2139